Matthew Clark

SERIAL
KILLERS

CANADA

**A Disturbing Journey in the Most Shocking True Crime Stories
in Canadian History**

Table Of Contents

Introduction

The word "serial" means or implies more than one crime, and the term "killer" implies a person who has killed at least three people with a "cooling-off period" in-between each murder. It is estimated that less than 1% of homicides involve serial killers.

How to Spot a Serial Killer?

They usually commit crimes near their home, are not very intelligent, and have problems with authority figures. Real serial killers are not always white, middle-class males. They do not always use a gun, don't jump out of the bushes and start shooting, and don't always have a motive.

It is estimated that serial killers kill an average of 10 people each, with approximately 550 victims in the United States all-time. Some serial killers leave clues at the crime scene; more intelligent serial killers rarely do so. There are no definitive physical characteristics of a serial killer because everyone is unique. Real serial killers tend to be very thorough at concealing evidence. If the crime had taken place years ago, there might not have been any physical evidence left.

Serial killers are very methodical and organized; they plan their crimes in advance and meticulously prepare for them. Some serial killers seek fame, and there is some evidence that these individuals welcome the opportunity to capture their crimes on audiotape or videotape. They sometimes keep souvenirs of their victims such as clothing, jewelry, or body parts (e.g., fingers).

How Do Serial Killers Get Started?

Most serial killers have been abused as children. Serial killers have most likely had a bad relationship with the opposite sex in their teen years, they were bullied as a child, and they seem to be easily manipulated while in prison.

Many serial killers are white males between the ages of 20 and 40. Members of their family abused many; many are loners or social misfits; some had no father figure in their lives, and some were very intelligent. Some serial killers are very athletic, but most are not. Often serial killers have a fascination or an obsession with police work and fire-fighting. Women abused an estimated 75% of serial killers.

What Motivates Serial Killers?

Most serial killers do not fit the stereotype of crazed maniacs who kill for pleasure. Instead, they are usually mature individuals who kill for material gain or want to fulfill their own personal psychological needs. A need for power drives some serial killers, an obsession with authority drives some, and some kill for the thrill of it.

Many serial killers are white males between the ages of 20 and 40. Often they have been abused by women in their youth; they can be loners or social misfits. Some were very intelligent. Many had no father figure in their lives; some were very aggressive as children and turned to crime to make up for it; some see violence as a way to relieve frustration.

The motivation of serial killers usually changes over time. Most serial killers start out killing animals and work their way up to humans. Some serial killers do not have trouble controlling their urges; others do. Some kill people and steal from their homes; these are called "organized" killers, while others kill for pleasure and leave behind "impulse" murders. Some murderers are driven by a need for power, some by an obsession with authority, and some kill for the thrill of it; they do not plan or try to conceal evidence. They fear most the individual who is responsible for their capture.

Russell Williams

David Russell Williams was born on March 7, 1963. He is a former Colonel in the Canadian Forces and a convicted murderer and rapist. He was the former commander of Canadian Forces Base Trenton, the country's largest and busiest airfield and a center for air transport operations in Canada and overseas. Williams was also a renowned military pilot who has flown VIP planes for Canadian dignitaries such as the great Queen Elizabeth II, Prince Philip and the governor-general, the prime minister, and others.

Due to criminal allegations, he was removed from his base commander at CFB Trenton on February 8, 2010. Based on evidence gathered by the Ontario Provincial Police, he was formally charged by the Crown Attorney with two counts of first-degree murder, two counts of forcible confinement, two counts of breaking, and two counts of sexual assault; another 82 charges were later added for breaking.

In October 2010, Williams was sentenced to two life terms for first-degree murder, two ten-year sentences for additional sexual assaults, two ten-year sentences for forcible imprisonment, and 82 one-year sentences for burglary. All of the sentences will be completed at Kingston Penitentiary concurrently. Under the conditions of his life sentence, Williams must serve a minimum of 25 years before being eligible for parole. Williams is ineligible for early release under the "faint hope provision" of the Canadian Criminal Code since he has been sentenced of multiple murders.

On the advice of the Chief of the Defence Staff, the Governor-General of Canada stripped Williams of his commission, ranks, and medals on October 22, 2010. His severance compensation was canceled, and the money he earned after his arrest was confiscated, but he remains eligible for a pension. His uniform was burned, honors were destroyed, reputations were destroyed and wrecked as a result of his conviction.

Early Life

Cedric David Williams and Christine Nonie Williams raised Williams in Bromsgrove, England. His family came to Canada and settled in Chalk River, Ontario. His father got a job as a metallurgist at Chalk River Laboratories, Canada's leading nuclear research facility.

After coming to Chalk River, the Williams family met the Sovkas, and they became fast friends. The families would spend a significant amount of time together. Williams' parents separated when he was six years old, and Nonie Williams married Jerry Sovka soon after. Williams adopted his stepfather Dr. Jerry Sovka's surname during this period and relocated to Scarborough, Ontario. Williams started secondary school at Toronto's Birchmount Collegiate but ended at Upper Canada College while living in the Scarborough Bluffs. He delivered The Globe and Mail and studied the piano. By 1979, he and his family had relocated to South Korea, where Sovka was in charge of another nuclear project. While his parents were in South Korea, Williams finished his last two years of high school at Toronto's Upper Canada College. In his last year, 1982, he was elected as one of two boarding house prefects and reported to his house steward, Andrew Saxton, who is currently the Conservative Member of Parliament for North Vancouver.

He married Mary Elizabeth Harriman, an associate director of the Heart and Stroke Foundation of Canada, on June 1, 1991. According to his Canadian Defense Department biography, Williams is an enthusiastic shutterbug, fisherman, and sprinter. He and his wife Mary are also passionate golfers.

Trouble Life as a Serial Killer

Colonel David Russell Williams was a deviant, a cross-dressing burglar who broke into homes to take photos of himself in women's underwear. He was also a rapist, his nighttime ramble inexorably leading to sexual violence. Finally, he was a murderer, claiming two victims and recording their killings on film and in photos that would establish him as one of Canada's most heinous killers.

Williams' first military assignment was at Portage la Prairie, which is located just west of Winnipeg. In 1991, while stationed there, he married Mary Elizabeth Harriman. He was promoted to captain and moved to Canadian Forces Base Shearwater in Nova Scotia a year later. In 1999, he was endorsed to major, and four years later, he was promoted to lieutenant colonel. He'd earned a master's degree in defense studies from the Royal Military College in the interim.

Williams' military career flourished, and he spent six months in 2005/06 at Camp Mirage, a covert station in Dubai that provides logistical assistance to Canadian soldiers in Afghanistan. In 2009, he was chosen commanding officer of CFB Trenton, Canada's biggest air force installation, with 2,300 air force troops under his charge.

Williams and his wife, Elizabeth, were spending their time between two residences by this point. Their primary address was an upscale home in Ottawa's fashionable Westboro Village. On Cosy Cove Lane in Tweed, there was also a lakeside holiday house. Williams usually remained alone during the week because it was considerably closer to the air force base. It left him with a lot of free time.

Williams eventually confessed that he began breaking into his neighbors' homes in 2007. The first incursions happened in September of that year, while neighbors Ron and Monique Murdoch and their children were visiting Monique's mother in neighboring Sudbury.

Williams entered the residence through an unlocked door and went to the 12-year-old Murdoch's daughter's room. He spent three hours there, trying on the girl's undergarments and photographing himself. He walked away with six of her underwear and bras.

Over the next three years, Williams would return to the girl's chamber twice more while also invading the homes of 47 other neighbors and meticulously recording these incursions. On each time, he'd follow a strict pattern, photographing the underwear in the drawer first, then piling it onto a bed, shooting individual things, then trying on some of the clothes and photographing himself. Then he'd go, typically with several pairs of underpants.

It's worth noting that most sex offenders begin while they're young and then taper off by the time they're in their forties. On the other hand, Williams had no history of sexual deviance until 2007, when he was 44 years old. Several ideas have been advanced to explain this, one of which being that he was administered

Prednisone for the first time that year to manage chronic discomfort. Manic behavior and even psychotic illnesses have been related to the drug.

That notion is countered by the fact that Williams continued to fly military planes, and therefore his exposure to powerful medicines like Prednisone would have been tightly controlled. It's also worth noting that none of Williams' neighbors observed any difference in his conduct. He was still considered a nice neighbor and a decent citizen, and he was friendly with many of the people whose right to privacy he was infringing.

If that had been the whole of Russell Williams' misdeeds, he might not have been apprehended. His misdeeds, however, intensified in September 2009 when he attacked two women.

The first of these events occurred just after midnight on September 16, 2009, when Williams broke into a household just a few blocks from his lakeside home in Tweed. He'd been checking out the place for a while, so he knew a young woman and her infant daughter resided there. He assaulted the woman while she was watching TV with the flashlight he was holding. Then he tied her up, blinded her, and started sexually abusing her. He promised she wouldn't be raped. He was only looking to snap some pictures. He then began filming the nude woman before shooting himself in her underpants. He donned a black ski mask during the attack.

Only two weeks later, Williams assaulted another lady, this time just a few blocks from his home. He sexually abused (but did not rape) the woman once again. He took photographs once more.

The woman later misidentified her assailant as another neighbor, Larry Jones, which resulted in Jones' imprisonment. After willingly submitting to a polygraph test and providing a blood sample, he was released, which exonerated him of the crime. Colonel Russell Williams, on the other hand, was on his way to murder.

Corporal Marie-France Comeau worked as a flight attendant on military Airbus A-310s that carried the prime minister and other guests. She was a flight attendant on a flight bringing Prime Minister Stephen Harper to Mumbai, India, in November 2009. On November 25, after returning from her long-distance journey, she retreated to her house on Raglan Street in Brighton. Unbeknownst to her, an intruder was hidden behind a heater in her home.

Williams had intended to attack Comeau after she had gone to bed. When she walked downstairs seeking her cat, he took advantage of the situation, hitting the 38-year-old lady with his flashlight and tied her to a pole.

He hauled in a lot of lamps, illuminating the space so that he could record himself. At the same time, he raped her, elaborating on his previous M.O. During the rape, Comeau began pleading for her life, and Williams wrapped her mouth and nose with duct tape, forcing her to pass out. He then dragged her upstairs and raped her once again.

Williams believed he heard a disturbance at this moment and proceeded to investigate. During his absence, Comeau freed herself and nearly fled. Williams apprehended her as she attempted to flee to the restroom. He beat her with the flashlight before strangling her to death. He then removed the shackles and duct tape he'd taken with him and took them away from the site. He hadn't been as cautious as he'd hoped. He'd left a footprint in Marie's blood.

Marie-France Comeau's body was discovered the next day by her lover. Williams, as her commanding officer, wrote the official letter of condolence to her father. Jessica Lloyd, 27, did not show up for work at Tri-Board Student Transportation Services on January 29, 2010. When she failed to call in, coworkers grew concerned and attempted to contact her. When they received no response, they notified her relatives, who went to check on her. Jessica wasn't at home, but her family was concerned about something. Her purse was close to her car in the driveway. They contacted the cops because they suspected something was wrong.

While authorities searched for the missing woman, her assailant, Colonel Russell Williams, was flying a military plane to California. By the time Williams went to work on February 4, the police had put up a roadblock on his usual route. Williams' Pathfinder SUV was one of the cars hauled over that day, with cops making a huge deal out of inspecting his tires. Three days later, on Sunday, February 7, Williams received a call at his Ottawa townhouse summoning him to police headquarters for interrogation.

At first, Williams was arrogant, smirking and joking with his interrogator, Inspector Jim Smyth. His mood shifted, though, once Smyth cut to the chase. They knew Williams was at Jessica Lloyd's house on the night of January 29, he claimed. An off-duty cop had spotted a Pathfinder parked there, and the tire tracks left behind were identical to his.

Backed into a position, Williams quickly confessed, claiming that he did so to rescue his wife from the shame of a lengthy police inquiry.

In relation to the Lloyd murder, Williams stated that he saw Jessica working out on a treadmill in her basement one morning while out on the run (he often used these runs to potential case victims). A few nights later, while Jessica was sleeping, he broke in, tied, gagged, and blinded her, then raped her, all while filming and photographing everything. He then drove her from her house to his cabin, where he continued to attack her.

The recording of the attack, which was eventually recovered by authorities, is horrific to see. Jessica is spotted in the bathtub nude and trembling. She begs Williams to take her to the hospital, claiming she is dying. Williams later forced Jessica to appear in lingerie for him as he took reel after reel of photos. Finally, he bludgeoned her to death with the flashlight before strangling her. Her corpse was discovered along a rural road not far from his property. The cops would locate her on February 8 if they followed Williams' instructions.

On October 18, 2010, David Russell Williams pled guilty to two charges of murder, two counts of sexual assault, and 82 counts of burglary during his trial. He was sentenced to two life sentences in prison for murder and 120 years in total for the other offenses. His military rank, decorations, and honors were later revoked. Williams is being detained in solitary confinement at a maximum-security prison in Kingston, Ontario. He will be 72 years old when he is eligible for release in 2035.

Daniel Wood

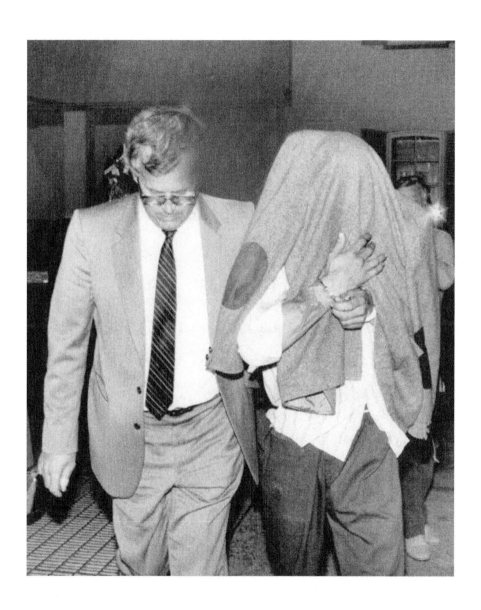

Daniel William Wood, like most serial killers, had a shady start in life. Wood was born in British Columbia in 1955, the son of a heroin-addicted prostitute who died when he was twelve years old. Wood had already been on the streets for two years, having run away at the age of 10 and supported himself via small stealing. This invariably got him into a confrontation with the law, and the youngster spent most of his childhood being shuttled between various juvenile institutions. He eventually progressed to adult jails.

Wood felt it was time for a change in pastures in 1979. He bought a Greyhound ticket and headed east to Calgary. Shortly after his arrival in that city, authorities discovered a homeless lady's raped and strangled body in an alleyway, buried behind an abandoned vehicle. Suspicion fell on a stranger who had been seen in the woman's company, but Danny Wood fled town before the police could investigate.

Wood next appeared at Smith's Falls, a tiny hamlet near Ottawa. A disabled lady alleged a rape by a man matching Woods' description during his brief time there. Woods, once again, did not stay long enough to answer questions. He was on his way to North Bay, Ontario. Death was unavoidable.

Claude Oulette returned to the North Bay house he lived with his girlfriend, Micheline St. Armour, on July 10, 1980. When Micheline didn't respond to his greetings, he proceeded in search of her, coming to a halt in the bedroom when he spotted a trail of blood. The path led to a cupboard, which Claude cautiously opened. Micheline's nude body was crammed within, blood seeping from multiple puncture wounds. An autopsy revealed that she had been stabbed 27 times. She, too, had been raped.

Despite initial hopes of a speedy arrest in the St. Armour murder, the trail quickly fell cold. Meanwhile, another tragedy happened only a few miles north along Highway 11 in New Liskard, Ontario. Julie Fortier, eighteen, alighted from a school bus on September 19, 1980, soon vanished. Julie remained unidentified until 1990 when her decomposing remains were discovered at an informal landfill outside of town despite a concerted search.

But it was in the far future. The ghost of death still plagued the villages along Highway 11 in the present. Sharon McCafferty, 32, a part-time prostitute, was discovered in a hotel room in Timmins, Ontario, on October 7. Her murderer had cut open her chest in a jagged cross design after she'd been raped and strangled. Danny Wood was a worker in the region at the time, and after a witness identified him as being in McCafferty's company on the night she died, he was arrested and charged with her murder. However, he was acquitted at trial, and detectives failed to notice the stunning connections to other killings in the region.

In the spring of 1982, Wood was in Toronto when Jenny Isford, 19, was raped and strangled, and her corpse was found in a neighbor's yard. Christine Prince's corpse was recovered in a forested area on the Rouge River's bank less than a month later. A third body, Judy Anne Delisle, was discovered as authorities became concerned about the potential of a serial murderer operating in the region. She had been raped, strangled, and sexually disfigured, just like the previous victims. This time, though, a witness came forward with a precise description of the murderer. That description ultimately led investigators to Danny Wood.

Wood was tried, convicted, and sentenced to life in prison for the Delisle murder. And things could have ended there if Wood hadn't alerted prison officials in August 1982. He had some important information to give, according to Wood. Fernand Robinson, his cellmate, had boasted to him about the fifteen killings he had committed. Robinson had detailed the killings in great detail, which Wood revealed, including information that only the killer would know. The main flaw in Wood's account was that Robinson was in prison when most of the killings were committed. That left only one explanation for how Wood knew so much about the murders. He was the one who had committed them.

Danny Wood has never been prosecuted for any of the killings he recounted, even though authorities believe he is responsible for at least fifteen violent fatalities. He is still imprisoned in a maximum-security institution in Saskatchewan.

Robert Pickton

On October 24, 1949, Robert "Willie" Pickton was born on his family's pig farm in Port Coquitlam, British Columbia. His life was tough from the start; it is believed that he was born with his umbilical cord securely wrapped around his throat, robbing him of vital air as the midwife battled to cut him free.

His parents thought that the incident had resulted in learning difficulties and potentially irreparable brain damage. Many years later, his defense team seized on this issue as well, providing an IQ test that allegedly revealed very poor intelligence. Even if Pickton wasn't a genius—even if he did suffer from brain damage—no one could deny that he was a tough young man.

He grew raised in some tough circumstances. Pickton's parents' primitive farm didn't always have running water, and as a child, he remembers pulling up the floorboard under his bed to get to the pure spring water that ran beneath. In this challenging atmosphere, Robert Pickton appears to have developed into a self-starter, learning and doing things at a much younger age than typical, including driving the family truck at the age of three.

Pickton recounts being left alone in his father's antique Maple Leaf truck, a Canadian/General Motors classic from the 1940s. He leaped into the driver's seat with zeal and inadvertently shifted the car into neutral. The truck lunged ahead, sending pigs flying as it careened down the steep ground, until Pickton, frightened, drove the vehicle directly into a telephone pole. His father "beat the crap" out of him when he was dragged from the damaged truck. His father didn't seem to mind that he'd been messing around or even driving the truck—he was simply furious that he'd smashed it!

Pickton's mother and father appear to have taken an unorthodox approach to child-rearing in general. Just a year after this occurrence, his mother found him smoking a cigarette—and her method of treating him was to offer him a cigar! Yes, she pushed her four-year-old kid to smoke himself sick by stuffing a stogie down his throat. It worked, to be sure; Pickton never wanted to smoke again.

Robert Pickton's childhood occurred long before Child Protective Services began swooping down on the smallest deviation in childcare. Pickton was totally at the mercy of his mother and father, Leonard and Louise because no outside authority kept an eye on him.

Locals would recall the extreme strangeness of Louise Pickton in particular for many years after the occurrence. Her habits were obviously unsanitary, with a mouth full of rotting teeth, an almost hairless head (save for a few mousy strands hidden by a bandanna), and a face with a fuzzy beard emerging from its surface. Apparently unconcerned about her appearance, Louise would brazenly march out of the home in a dress and boots, yelling at the top of her lungs to Robert and his brothers, "Git over here—now!!"

Robert was his mother's major target, and she was continually berating and directing him. His father, a British immigrant who had come to Canada as a young man, had a more remote parenting style, preferring to remain aloof.

Life on the Picktons' pig farm was difficult. The children were always cleaning up after the animals, which comprised a few cows and nearly 200 piglets. Pig farms, of course, are notorious for their foul odors, and the Pickton farm allegedly ranked high on the list of stinky pig farms. The family could never remove the odor completely, and the children were frequently mocked for the odor that accompanied them. The Pickton youngsters were generally known as the "Piggies" among the neighborhood brats. His brothers accepted the unoriginal title in stride and soon forgot about it, but the childhood insult would sting for many years to come for Robert.

Robert Pickton began attending Millside, the local primary school when he was six years old. Pickton was obviously uncomfortable and bashful with his peers because he had received no formal training in etiquette or social interaction at home. As a result, his exam results deteriorated, and he received poor ratings in nearly every subject. His second year in school was not much better than the first, and it was decided that he would have to be held back a grade in order to catch up with his contemporaries. When he eventually made it to third grade, he was sent to the closest approach to a special needs class that 1950s Canada offered. He would spend the remainder of his time in school in special education classes.

Pickton enrolled at Mary Hill Secondary School when he was 13 years old, but he finally quit school owing to the tremendous criticism he continued to suffer for his unpleasant odor and lack of intelligence. Playground bullies regularly targeted Pickton, and the strain pushed him to drop out of school for good. And, just as society had rejected Pickton, Pickton would soon reject society completely.

Donald Sherman Staley

The 4th of July, 1946, was a beautiful day in Vancouver, British Columbia, the type of day made for swimming. Garry Billings, 11, and Bobby Sherman, 8, decided to make the most of the pleasant weather. The two set out for Stanley Park Beach early that morning. They spent hours frolicking in the surf before retreating to a shaded place on the beach to recuperate before returning to the waves.

Garry and Bobby had just found a position to rest on the busy beach when a young soldier in full uniform took up a spot near them, despite the heat of the day. Because the man was kind, the lads eagerly accepted his offer to buy them ice cream. They spent the remainder of the afternoon talking with the man, who told them combat experiences. When an RCMP officer approached the group, the soldier identified himself as Donald Staley and stated that he had recently been dismissed from the Scottish military. The officer left, apparently happy with the man's objectives. After a time, Garry and Bobby announced they had to go.

Staley sent them to go with a few coins and invited them to meet him on the beach at noon the next day.

The boys were eager to see their new buddy again, and when Bobby arrived at his friend's house the next day, he discovered that Garry had already departed. Despite his disappointment, Bobby continued to the shore, where he planned to meet up with his friend. But Garry was nowhere to be seen, and neither was the nice soldier they had met the day before. Bobby ultimately returned home after an unsuccessful hunt. In the days that followed, a major hunt for Garry Billings began. It eventually failed. It seemed as if the sea had sucked up the child.

Another kid went missing nineteen days after Garry Billings, this time from St. George Island in Calgary, some 600 miles distant. Donnie Goss, six, was playing with a group of youngsters when a guy drew him away. This time, the police hunt resulted in a fast but sad end. Within 24 hours, Donny's body was discovered in bushes near the playground. He'd been savagely beaten, choked, cut, and stabbed. There were additional indications of sexual assault, both before and after the victim's death.

On July 24, Vancouver police made a sad find of their own. The corpse of Garry Billings was discovered in a shallow burial in Stanley Park. He had been beaten and stabbed to death, and there was evidence of both rape and necrophilia, as in the Goss case. The soldier who had talked to Garry and Bobby the day before Garry's abduction drew instant notice from the police. Fortunately, the RCMP policeman knew who he was - Donald Staley.

Staley, it turned out, was not difficult to locate. He was detained in Calgary during a restaurant burglary and was presently being held at the Lethbridge prison. Detectives from Vancouver rushed straight to the jail to interview him, arriving on August 17. In reality, they had little strong proof against Staley and were bracing themselves for difficult questioning. Staley, to their astonishment, confessed almost quickly to murdering

Garry Billings. Then, almost as an afterthought, he admitted to murdering Donnie Goss as well.

Staley stated that he encountered Garry on the beach about 11:50 a.m. and convinced him to accompany him to the adjacent park. He had persuaded Garry into going into the bushes by promising him a dollar. He'd started sexually abusing the youngster once he was away from inquisitive eyes. Staley strangled Garry senseless, then stabbed him to death with a four-inch paring knife when he struggled. He placed the child's corpse in a hollow after indulging in postmortem intercourse with it, then covered it with logs and bushes.

Staley used a similar ploy to separate Donnie Goss from his playmates in the case of Donnie Goss. He hit the child on the back of the head with a handmade cosh, some buckshot enclosed in a sock, once he was in the bushes. The sock, however, split on impact and barely startled the youngster. Donnie then started fighting for his life, displaying incredible strength for a six-year-old. Staley's troubles came to an end with a stab to the heart. As he lay dying, he had intercourse with the kid. Staley didn't even try concealing the body this time.

On Monday, September 30, 1946, Donald Staley went on trial in Calgary. He filed a temporary insanity plea, claiming his difficult background as a mitigating factor. And Staley's youth did appear to be a blueprint for the development of a serial sex offender. Staley, who was born out of wedlock, never met his father and was left an orphan when his mother died when he was three years old. The Ansty family adopted him after two years, but he would spend the following six years in and out of supervised care due to his chronic thieving. During these years of detention, he was sexually molested regularly by older convicts. Staley joined the army at the age of sixteen and was deployed overseas. However, because of his disobedience and illegal activities, he spent as much time in incarceration as he did on active service.

Staley stated on the evidence that he had had cruel sexual fantasies involving children since he was a teenager. On the day he assaulted Garry Billings, those imaginations had taken possession of him. He stated that he had passed out during the strikes and could only recall a few details.

Staley's voice was trembling, and he occasionally burst into tears as he gave his evidence. The jurors, on the other hand, showed little compassion for Staley's pleadings for mercy. They eventually returned the judgment that everyone expected — guilty. After that, Staley was condemned to death by hanging.

Donald Sherman Staley was hanged on December 18, 1946. In the greatest public hanging in Canadian history, he was killed with four German prisoners of war.

Clifford Olson

Clifford Robert Olson was born on January 1, 1940. Many would say he was born under a terrible sign since he was frequently in trouble from a young age, a downward spiral that would culminate with him being, possibly, Canada's greatest despised serial murderer. Clifford Jr., the eldest of Clifford and Leona Olson's four children, grew raised in Vancouver and Richmond. He was a small, stocky boy who was often bullied until he decided to take up boxing and turn the tables on his tormentors. He subsequently turned into a bully himself.

Despite being a bright young man, he struggled in school, dropping out in the eighth grade and plunging into a life of crime. Olson was sentenced to his first prison term in July 1957, at the age of 17, and spent the next 24 years in and out of prison for a variety of offenses ranging from forgery to breaking and entering to sexual assault. He escaped from custody seven times.

Olson was released from yet another term of imprisonment in January 1980. A few months later, he began seeing Joan Hale, a divorcee. In April 1981, the couple gave birth to a son, Stephen, and married a month later. By then, Olson had already begun the murdering rampage that would establish him as one of the most heinous serial killers of all time.

Christine Weller, a 12-year-old girl from Richmond, British Columbia, was Olson's first victim, taken from her home on November 19, 1980. Her corpse was discovered on Christmas Day, more than a month later. She'd received ten severe stab wounds in her chest and belly, including one that slashed through her heart and liver.

Colleen Daignault, at thirteen, was apprehended on South Surrey street on April 15, 1981. Olson drove her to a distant location and murdered her with a hammer. He enticed Daryn Johnsrude from a shopping center in New Westminster and took him to Deroche less than a week later. The 16-year-old was sodomized before being brutally bludgeoned with a hammer.

The disappearance of three youngsters in the same geographical region in such a short period of time sparked concern. Despite this, the cops looked unconcerned, maintaining that the children had run away from home.

When Sandra Lynn Wolfsteiner, 16, went missing on May 19, 1981, they adhered to that line. Olson had taken Sandra from a bus station in Surrey to a secluded spot near Chilliwack Lake. When Sandra's body was discovered, an autopsy indicated that she died due to severe blunt force trauma, most likely caused by a hammer.

Ada Anita Court, 13, went missing on June 21, 1981, after failing to come home from a babysitting job. Olson had picked her up on Coquitlam's North Road. He'd driven her to Weaver Lake, raped her, and then bludgeoned her to death. Simon Patrick Partington, Olson's youngest victim, was just nine years old when

Olson kidnapped him off a Richmond street, drove him to a secluded location, and strangled him. On July 2, Olson persuaded 14-year-old Judy Kozma into his car and drove her to Weaver Lake, where he raped and stabbed her to death.

The police's "runaway" hypothesis was in shambles by this point, and with the media and concerned public demanding action, the RCMP compiled a list of probable suspects. Clifford Olson was one of the names on the list, and he was placed under intermittent monitoring. Despite the fact that over 200 policemen were assigned to the investigation, the authorities were unable to put a halt to his deadly rampage.

Raymond Lawrence King Jr., 15, died on July 23, 1981, at Weaver Lake. Olson had picked him up at the Westminster bus station, enticing him with the promise of construction employment. Once in the car, Olson handed the teenager a chloral hydrate-laced soft drink. Raymond was sodomized after passing out, then thrown down an embankment and beaten to death with a rock.

Sigrun Arnd, a German student, was hitchhiking in Coquitlam on July 24 when Olson stopped to give her a lift. He drove her to Richmond, his favorite killing site, and bludgeoned her to death. Two days later, he raped and strangled Terry Lyn Carson, 15, near Chilliwack.

Finally, on July 30, 1981, Olson picked up Louise Chartrand, 17, as she walked to work in Maple Ridge, British Columbia. He drove her to Whistler, where he raped and murdered her.

Olson was speeding up, killing his final three victims in less than a week. It's terrifying to think of how much more devastation he could have inflicted if he'd stayed at large. Fortunately, on July 31, police chose to arrest him as he was picking up two female hitchhikers on Vancouver Island.

Even with their main suspect in custody, the cops had very little evidence to work with. Olson might have walked away from the accusations if he hadn't given investigators a bargain. In exchange for $100,000, he'd give out the location of the bodies as well as a confession to each of the killings.

Of fact, paying for information is a part of police operations all over the world. This was, however, unprecedented. The perpetrator of the offenses was looking to benefit from them in this case. The authorities were forced to make an unenviable decision: pay the money or let a horrible killer walk free, most likely to kill again. In the end, Attorney General Allan Williams consented to the agreement, thus ending his political career.

Olson's reaction was to call his wife Joan and say, "Honey, you're going to be rich."

A convoy of police vehicles, including dog teams and forensic specialists, set off towards the forest-clad slopes of British Columbia, with the money held in trust until Olson fulfilled his end of the bargain. Olson took them to one decaying corpse after another over the following few days, explaining with delight what he'd done to his victims. A six-inch spike had been hammered into the skull of one of the children. In another case, Olson injected an air bubble into the victim's vein to cause an embolism.

Clifford Olson went on trial in January 1982 and pleaded guilty to all counts leveled against him. On January 11, he was sentenced to eleven concurrent life sentences, bringing an end to one of Canada's deadliest serial murder cases.

But the investigation was far from done. The media disclosures that Olson had been paid for his confession sparked outrage. In the aftermath, Attorney General Williams was forced to retire, and legal action was launched to get Joan Olson to repay the $100,000 she was paid. It failed, and pleas to Mrs. Olson's conscience fell on deaf ears for many years. She argued that she was just as much a victim as any dead children and so deserved the money.

Meanwhile, Clifford Olson continued to communicate with the press and call radio talk shows from behind bars. He wrote nasty letters and greeting cards to the victims' parents, bragging about what he'd done to their children. He sent obscene letters to members of the House of Commons. He repeatedly petitioned the parole board for early release. And, like many of his contemporaries, he claimed additional killings, ranging from 30 to 134 depending on his mood.

We'll never know if such assertions are genuine or not. Clifford Olson passed away from cancer on October 2, 2011. He was 71 years old at the time.

Bruce McArthur

Bruce was renowned as a gentleman—a diligent worker who was kind and always obeyed the rules. But this man, who claimed to cherish law and order, had a turbulent and uncertain existence. His 20-year marriage ended in the late 1990s as he slowly and laboriously came out as a gay man. His lifestyle changed fast after that, not only in terms of sexual orientation but also in terms of geography. He transitioned from the rural limitations of small-town Canada to the metropolitan fervor of the country's largest metropolis, Toronto.

Here, he earned a mixed reputation as a charmer, a slick talker, and a man with a short temper, ready to erupt into full-fledged wrath at any time. Some of McArthur's associates just cannot believe he is guilty of the atrocities he is now accused of. Others, however, believe that Bruce McArthur had "serial murderer" written all over him.

To be clear, before anybody in the court of public opinion wrongly seeks to seal this man's doom, McArthur has yet to have his day in court as of this writing. He has only been accused; he has not yet been proven guilty of any crime.

Bruce McArthur, the alleged killer who has lately made headlines in Toronto, was born in Woodville, Ontario, on October 8, 1951. Woodville is a 650-person hamlet in the Kawartha Lakes area, a lush valley of farms and fields about 70 miles north of Toronto. Woodville was mostly known for its railroad stations and cheese factory, not for alleged serial murders until this year.

Malcolm and Islay McArthur, Bruce's parents, were well-respected community members who managed a small family farm that occasionally functioned as a foster home for troublesome kids. At any given time, the McArthurs were caring for up to ten foster children. Bruce attended a school that appeared more appropriate to 1800s frontier life than the stereotypically suburban 1950s here in the pastoral serenity of small-town Ontario.

The one-room schoolhouse on the outskirts of Woodville where Bruce learned the fundamentals of reading, writing, and arithmetic couldn't have been more rustic in character. The ancient schoolhouse has now been converted into a single-family home, but it was here that Bruce McArthur received his education during his youth and adolescence.

His old classmates were startled to learn of his imprisonment. They all stated that they had no recollection of anything unusual about his behavior at school. Far from being a delinquent, the Bruce McArthur they knew was a prim and proper goody-two-shoes who never got involved in his friends' misbehavior. Several students remember him as a teacher's pet and tattletale. McArthur was the one who informed school officials on several occasions when students were misbehaving or planning pranks.

It beggars comprehension for those who grew up in Woodville and spent their formative years with Bruce in that one-room schoolhouse that he could be charged of injuring anybody, let alone being a serial murderer! Bruce's character does not appear to have had any propensity toward violence or hostility in these early days. He played by the rules, but not maliciously, and he was regarded as a charmer with a gifted set of vocal cords who frequently competed in local singing contests.

Bruce ultimately transferred from Woodville's one-room schoolhouse to Fenelon Falls Secondary School. Fenelon Falls offered both a four-year and a five-year program. The four-year diploma concentrated largely on technical and creative occupations, and Bruce chose this route for himself. His friends at Fenelon Falls had only positive recollections of him, and former classmates were startled and disappointed to learn of his imprisonment. Marion Clark Luchies' response told it all as she said, "No! I can't believe it!"

So McArthur got along well in Fenelon Falls, where he met his future wife, Janice Campbell. Both graduated with honors in 1970, but the comment beneath Janice Campbell's yearbook photo appears comical in retrospect—she identified her number-one pet hate as "someone who can't determine what they want." It was a portent of things to come for the future wife of Bruce McArthur, a man who would one day break their marriage with a sudden shift in his sexual orientation.

Janice Campbell became Mrs. McArthur, and the young couple relocated to Toronto to start a new life. They didn't have steady work or a high-paying position in Canada's largest city, but they grabbed what they could and made the best of it. Their tenacity finally paid off, and McArthur got a small position at Eaton's, a downtown department store.

It's worth noting that at the time, Canada's "Gay Village"—a social hub for Canadian LGBT people—was taking root in the neighborhood of this department store. In the early 1970s, the neighborhood was already thriving on Yonge Street, College and Wellesley. However, it is unclear if McArthur took a special interest in this up-and-coming region that was almost next door to his job or whether it was simply a coincidence that he worked there.

Worryingly, inexplicable killings and disappearances occurred in the area about the time McArthur came on the scene. To be sure, this might be just another coincidence, but many people are openly wondering about McArthur's involvement.

According to all accounts, Bruce and Janice led a peaceful married existence at this time. McArthur's employee, John Foot, has come forward with some insight into what McArthur was like at the time. Foot, a former vice-principal who was startled to learn of

McArthur's arrest, recalls him as a perfectly pleasant, amiable, and sociable man who never shown any aggressiveness or rage and got along well with everyone he met. Foot also met Janice, and after seeing the young married couple interact, he came away with the feeling that their marriage was genuinely happy.

The couple's sole major stumbling block came in 1978 when McArthur's mother died of a brain hemorrhage. He was heartbroken by the loss, which was exacerbated by his father's death a few years later, in 1981. Life moved on, and the couple eventually bought their first home together and had two children, Todd and Melanie. Friends, friends, and neighbors claim the family was the spitting image of normalcy throughout their time at the huge brick house in suburban Oshawa, located on Lake Ontario's coast.

Along with a lovely new home, McArthur had started a new job as a traveling salesman for McGregor Socks.

This work required McArthur to leave for extended periods of time to go from town to town—and although most young husbands and dads would despise being away from home, McArthur appeared to love it. This important aspect has prompted some to speculate that McArthur may have participated in murderous behavior throughout his sales route, implying that his victim list would be far longer than now stated. But before we start pointing fingers, connecting the connections, and getting on the serial killer bandwagon, let's take a step back, take a big breath, and look at the facts. As of this writing, McArthur has not been convicted of murder. Thus all of the information is speculative.

Aside from unproven misconduct claims, what we do know for certain about McArthur's existence as a traveling salesman is that he was very good at it. He quickly rose to prominence, and he was soon selling his products throughout much of Ontario. He was doing so well that he employed extra assistance as "counters" for his ever-expanding supply of socks and underwear. This group of slackers was tasked with tracking, planning, and ordering products for the expanding firm.

McArthur was utterly meek and gentle, a "sort of Caspar Milquetoast person" (referring to an old comic strip character of similar thinking), yet this mild-mannered salesman was also a true go-getter, according to John Foot. McArthur's commercial acumen and contacts allowed him to collaborate with well-known Sears and Hudson's Bay shops.

Unfortunately for the McArthurs, the good times didn't continue, and McArthur's sock and underwear empire fell altogether in 1993. McArthur was now fighting to make ends meet, and his prospects for the future were bleak. In the midst of his father's financial difficulties, his son Todd developed the unsettling habit of pranking unsuspecting individuals with obscene phone calls.

Initially, the family dismissed these activities as the juvenile conduct of a bored adolescent. However, the phone calls proved to be a far stronger temptation than anybody had anticipated. Todd continually kept phoning, no matter how many times he was told to stop. He appeared to be suffering from a serious addiction. As a result, he quickly ran out of warnings and was subjected to harsh legal repercussions in the shape of fines and restraining orders. The fines threw the McArthurs' finances into disarray, and they were compelled to mortgage their home in 1997.

Even though Bruce and Janice's marriage was clearly in trouble, they still managed to take at least one holiday. Glen Macleod, a caretaker, recounts meeting the couple in July 1997 while on vacation on Prince Edward Island. The trip had been organized by a relative of Macleod's who attended church with the couple. The woman reportedly felt terrible for the couple's recent difficulties, and she offered to let them stay for free at one of Macleod's summer houses.

The McArthurs accepted the kind offer and remained in the property for two nights, taking in the local sights throughout the day. Although the trip was a failure in terms of repairing their deteriorating marriage, McArthur left a favorable impression on Macleod, who remembers him as a "great gentleman" who appeared to be "soft-spoken and easygoing."

When Macleod saw on the news that a man he had met on Prince Edward Island in the late 1990s had been charged with numerous murders, he was stunned—and not just by the allegations. He was also taken aback by McArthur's overall look. McArthur, the man he'd known, was a clean, slender, and perfectly dressed man. The overweight, stocky, rough-and-tumble landscaper who began to stalk the pages of tabloid tabloids was unfamiliar to Macleod.

In any case, the McArthurs' visit to Prince Edward Island in 1997 was followed by bankruptcy in 1999. Against this backdrop, Bruce McArthur, a family man, quietly began to open the door to the private closet he had long locked himself inside.

Gerald Archer

Between 1969 and 1971, a nasty predator was roaming the streets of London, Ontario, a murderer with a penchant for aged hotel maids. Jane Wooley, a 60-year-old chambermaid at the London House Hotel, was the first to fall victim to this deviant. On February 3, 1969, Wooley had just ended her shift and went to her York Street apartment when she heard a tap on the door. The man on the threshold was either known to her or naive enough to talk his way in, for there was no evidence of forced entry. Once inside, he pounced on his helpless victim, beating and stabbing her to death. He also attempted to rape her but was unsuccessful.

Jane Wooley had been a dependable employee, but when she didn't show up for work for many days without even a phone call, her bosses phoned the cops. A team was rushed to the York Street flat and discovered the brutalized corpse already decomposing. Her clothes had been ripped off, and the congealed blood spatters on the walls, ceiling, and draperies indicated that she had been savagely beaten. Despite the frantic nature of the attack, the assassin had been cautious not to leave any traces. The trail had gone cold within weeks, and detectives had moved on to more important concerns.

Two years have passed. Then, in September 1970, another hotel employee was brutally assaulted. Edith Authier, 57, resided in the town of Merlin and worked at the neighboring William Pitt Hotel. On September 5, a neighbor inquired about Authier since she hadn't seen her in a while and was concerned for her well-being. She discovered Edith's semi-naked body in a pool of blood on the floor. She'd been battered and stabbed to death. An autopsy would subsequently reveal that she, too, had been raped. As in the instance of Jane Wooley, there was no evidence of forced entrance, implying that Authier knew her assailant. The killer had left no additional clues, at least none that would be relevant until DNA profiling was discovered decades later.

Once again, the police investigation into the incident came to a screeching end. On January 23, 1971, the killer claimed a third victim, and the case remained deadlocked. Belva Russell, like the previous two ladies, worked as a chambermaid at a London hotel. The 56-year-old had been out with her lover at the neighborhood pubs on the night she died. He left her to change her clothing at one point throughout the evening. She was gone when he returned. When the boyfriend inquired about Russell's whereabouts, he discovered that she had gone with a man. He went to her apartment to find her and got more than he bargained for. Belva Russell was found dead on the floor, her blood splattered on every surface in the flat, and her still-warm corpse ravished.

The murderer, on the other hand, had made a critical error this time. Customers at the pub had seen him leave with Russell, and many knew who he was. Gerald Thomas Archer, a minor criminal with a long police record for theft and burglary, was apprehended within hours.

Archer was charged with Belva Russell's murder, but despite the obvious similarities to the other two killings, the authorities failed to draw the link for whatever reason. Archer was later convicted and sentenced to life in prison. As he was escorted out of the courtroom, he said cryptically, "That's one strike against me." "The game isn't over yet!"

Gerald Archer would serve only 15 years of his life sentence before being released in 1985. Over the following decade, he moved from place to town, mostly staying out of trouble. At the age of 64, he died of a heart attack in 1995.

However, the narrative does not finish there. After his death, Archer's wife and daughter contacted police, claiming that he had acknowledged that he had murdered Edith Authier. Armed with this knowledge, authorities excavated Authier's remains and used DNA tests to confirm his identity. Archer was also connected by DNA to the death of Jane Wooley, putting the investigation of the London Chambermaid Killer to an end.

Paul Bernardo & Karla Homolka

On August 27, 1964, Paul Kenneth Bernardo was born into a wealthy family in Toronto, Ontario. Marilyn, his mother, was the adopted daughter of a rich Toronto lawyer, and Kenneth, his father, was the son of a well-to-do Italian businessman. Despite their affluent existence, things were not going well in the Bernardo home. Kenneth was a terrible man who beat his wife and sexually molested his own daughter. Marilyn was driven into the arms of a former boyfriend as a result of this abuse. She became pregnant with Paul as a result of her affair.

Kenneth Bernardo appears to have been surprisingly forgiving of his wife's adultery, given his regular aggression against her. He adopted the boy and listed himself as the biological father on Paul's birth certificate. Paul, for his part, looks unfazed by his chaotic family life. He grew up to be an attractive and well-adjusted young man who was courteous, good at school, and excited about his involvement in the Boy Scouts.

Everything changed in 1980 when Bernardo was 16, and his mother disclosed the truth about his origins to him. It severely harmed their relationship, and he publicly referred to her as "that whore" after that. Around this time, Paul began hanging out with a band of local bullies, and his attitude toward women began to deteriorate. He remained an excellent student, though, finishing high school and enrolling at Toronto University, where he finally graduated with a degree in accounting.

Paul Bernardo's life looked to be going swimmingly. But beneath the attractive young professional's exterior lay a deadly monster, a man who physically and mentally mistreated his female companions, a degenerate who made repeated demands for hard sex. Surprisingly, none of his girlfriends stayed for long. He didn't have any until he met Karla Homolka in October 1987.

Karla was blonde and beautiful, and unlike Bernardo's past lovers, she had no sexual depravity to which she would not go to satisfy her boyfriend. Nothing was off-limits. Paul asked Karla how she felt about his being a rapist shortly after their first encounter. It was "awesome," according to Karla.

The question wasn't just a trick of the tongue. Paul Bernardo had already committed three heinous rapes in the Scarborough region by the time he met Karla. He would wait at bus stations for a lone victim to come. He'd then come up behind her and grab her, threaten her with a knife, and pull her to a quiet location. He'd torture the unlucky woman to anal rape and forced fellatio there. Bernardo's attacks would frequently continue for more than an hour, during which time he would continually speak to his victim, reminding her how lucky she was to be raped by a gorgeous guy like him. At least eleven women would fall victim to the "Scarborough Rapist" before Bernardo moved to St. Catharines in May 1988, and the rapes abruptly ceased.

Bernardo's relationship with Homolka had progressed to the point that he had asked her to marry him by 1990. Karla was delighted to share the news with her parents, who were delighted with the union. Their prospective son-in-law was a young professional from a wealthy family who was attractive, well-spoken, and charming. The wedding was supposed to be one of the year's most social events. The Homolkas have beautiful grandkids to look forward to because of the couple's excellent looks.

There was just one flaw in that picture-perfect setting. Despite his twisted sexuality, Paul Bernardo desired a virginal wife. Karla had only had one sexual relationship before with him, but it wasn't enough for him. He threatened to call off the wedding, leaving

Karla heartbroken and afraid of losing the guy she adored. Karla was willing to listen when Paul proposed a remedy to the situation.

This was Bernardo's proposition. He hadn't taken Karla's virginity; thus, it was her obligation to supply him with a surrogate. Tammy, Karla's 15-year-old sister, was proposed by him. It was a heinous suggestion. Karla agreed without hesitation.

As a result, a strategy was devised. Karla would take halothane, an anesthetic medication, from the veterinary clinic where she worked. This would be used to knock Tammy unconscious, allowing Bernardo to rape her. The only issue was that the medication was often administered in gaseous form using a mask. Because they lacked this apparatus, they opted to soak the halothane in a towel and place it over Tammy's face.

Paul and Karla were at the Homolka house for a pre-Christmas meal on December 23, 1990. Bernardo had recently purchased a new camcorder, which he utilized to record the family celebration. Meanwhile, Karla plied her sister with sedative-laced rum-and-eggnog drinks. Tammy was asleep cold on the couch by the time the rest of the family went to bed.

Bernardo and Homolka waited until Karla's parents seemed to be asleep. Tammy was then taken from the sofa and transported to the basement. The unconscious adolescent was stripped nude before Bernardo raped her vaginally and anally while videotaping the crime. Karla pressed the halothane-soaked towel on Tammy's face as she stirred. Then Paul instructed Karla to do sexual activities on her sleeping sister while the camera was still filming. Karla was unquestioning in her obedience.

But then everything went wrong. Tammy began vomiting and choking on her vomit all of a sudden. Karla attempted to flip her onto her stomach, as she'd been taught at the veterinarian clinic. However, it was not working. Tammy was choking, and they lacked the necessary training to assist her. They soon knew they would need to contact an ambulance.

But there was evidence to conceal before they could do so. Time was wasted dressing Tammy and concealing the medications that had been used to sedate her. Tammy was already going blue by the time they dialed 911.

The sound of sirens outside Karla Homolka's front door startled her parents up. They raced downstairs, only to find their youngest daughter being taken out on a stretcher. Tammy was still breathing, but barely. She died shortly afterward in the hospital. Her death was ascribed to asphyxiation from her own vomit as a result of excessive alcohol consumption. No one dared to investigate the extensive chemical burns on her face produced by the halothane.

Paul Bernardo was devastated by Tammy's death, but not for the reasons you might expect. He was irritated at not having his sexual plaything and frequently chastised Karla for overdosing her sister with halothane. He began threatening to call off the engagement once more, which upset Karla more than her sister's death. She determined to locate a new victim for Paul since she didn't want to lose him.

She selected a teenager she had just recently met (identified in court transcripts only as Jane Doe). Jane admired Karla and looked up to her as a role model, so she gladly accepted when she was asked to dine at her house. Jane was plied with poisoned beverages and quickly passed out. Karla then contacted Paul and urged him to come over because she had a surprise for him. Bernardo was overjoyed when he spotted the lovely adolescent, even more so when he discovered she was still a virgin.

Paul urged Karla to sexually attack the sleeping girl as he kept the video rolling after undressing Jane. Then Paul took her virginity, which was all recorded on videotape. Jane slept the entire event. She awoke the next morning with a hangover and no recall of the previous night's events. Karla informed her that she had consumed too much alcohol and had passed out. Jane welcomed Paul as if he were meeting him for the first time when he arrived at the flat.

Karla's present to Paul (which she referred to as her wedding gift) helped to re-establish the marriage plans. The pair married in June 1991 in a spectacular ceremony at the historic Niagara-on-the-Lake chapel. The newlyweds were taken from the church in a carriage carried by white horses to an elaborate celebration at Queen's Landing, complete with champagne and a sit-down meal of veal-stuffed pheasant for 150 guests.

However, the honeymoon period was brief. Bernardo was driving a Burlington area in the early hours of Saturday, June 15, only days after the wedding, when he noticed 14-year-old Leslie Mahaffy roaming the streets. Leslie had been locked out of her house for failing to comply with her curfew. Bernardo paused to speak with her before drawing a knife and forcing the adolescent into his car.

Bernardo brought Leslie to his house, told her to strip, and then began recording the nude, blindfolded, and obviously scared girl. Karla had been sleeping, but Paul told her to sexually abuse the girl when she awoke, giving her explicit directions while filming the incident. Then Paul grabbed over and began raping and sodomizing Leslie as she screamed in agony.

On June 29, 1991, while canoeing on Lake Gibson, a guy noticed a concrete block in the water with what seemed to be pieces of flesh wrapped in it. With the assistance of a fisherman, the guy retrieved the block from the lake and was astounded to discover that the flesh was a human foot.

The police were summoned, and a check of the area revealed five additional blocks containing human remains. Leslie Mahaffy may be recognized by her unique dental braces.

Bernardo and Homolka were cruising for possible victims on April 16, 1992, when they saw 15-year-old Kristen French in a church parking lot. Karla stepped out of the car and asked the girl for directions. She was carrying a map, which she laid out on the bonnet of the automobile. Bernardo came up behind Kristen and pushed her into the car at knifepoint as she bent down to look at the map.

The depraved pair held Kristen hostage for the next two days, exposing her to one horrible perversion after another, all painstakingly documented on camera. Kristen cooperated with their every demand, realizing it was her last hope of life. She had been raped, sodomized, and beaten with sex toys and other items. She was coerced into having oral sex with both Bernardo and Homolka. Bernardo urinated and even attempted to defecate on her.

Kristen French stoically suffered all of this heinous torture, but it wasn't enough to rescue her. Her nude body was discovered in a ditch near Burlington on April 30, 1992. Because the corpse had not been disfigured, the authorities first failed to connect the murder to that of Leslie Mahaffy. They didn't have much chance of capturing the perpetrator because there was so little evidence at the crime site.

They had no idea that they'd previously let him slip through their fingers on many occasions. When the Scarborough rapes were at their climax in 1988, a composite was created based on the testimonies of many victims. It struck a striking similarity to Paul Bernardo, but for reasons unknown to them, the police withheld the sketch for two years before revealing it in May 1990. When they did, numerous individuals called in to identify Bernardo, but the police were so swamped with calls that the leads were never followed up on.

It wasn't until 1992, after another slew of tips, a policeman was assigned to question Bernardo. He voluntarily gave blood, hair, and saliva samples, but the Scarborough rapes stopped by then, so the investigation was no longer a priority, and the samples were not examined.

Bernardo's samples would not be matched to the Scarborough victims' sperm until February 1993. When the testing was completed, Bernardo was linked to at least three of the assaults.

Bernardo was now the main suspect in a string of heinous rapes. However, the cops questioned whether there was more to the case than that. They had begun to think that he was responsible for Leslie Mahaffy and Kristen French's killings. They'd get an opportunity to put that idea to the test in a matter of days.

Karla, who had been severely battered, came into a police station on February 26, 1993, and filed assault accusations against her husband. Detectives rushed her into an interrogation room and questioned her for the next five hours, sensing an opportunity. On the other hand, Karla gave nothing away, despite the two black eyes she was sporting, courtesy of Paul. But she was tense, and the cops could tell. Shortly after they freed her, Karla hired a lawyer and approached prosecutors, seeking a plea bargain. Paul Bernardo was arrested in mid-February and charged with the Scarborough rapes and the Mahaffy and French killings.

The trial of Paul Bernardo was finally held in mid-1995. The prosecution's case against him was substantial, and it featured a collection of videotapes showing his victims' rapes, as well as evidence from his estranged wife. Bernardo was convicted of two charges of first-degree murder on September 1, 1995, and sentenced to life in jail with no chance of release for the next 25 years. He was also labeled a dangerous offender, which means he is unlikely to ever be released.

Karla Homolka was permitted to plead guilty to manslaughter in return for her testimony. She was sentenced to 12 years in jail but was freed after only three years in 2005. Her present whereabouts are unknown, although she is always afraid someone will assassinate her for her role in the murders.

For his safety, Paul Bernardo spends his time at the maximum-security Kingston Penitentiary in a 4-by-8-foot cell, apart from the rest of the prison population. Despite these precautions, he has apparently been attacked on at least two occasions by fellow detainees.

Cody Legebokoff

Cody Legebokoff (Cody Alan Legebokoff), also known as The Country Boy Murderer, is a Canadian serial killer and rapist. Between 2009 and 2010, Legebokoff killed three ladies and a young girl in British Columbia, Canada. One person was named as a possible victim in the Highway of Tear's killings. On Nexopia, a Canadian social networking site, he went by the pseudonym 1CountryBoy. He is one of Canada's youngest serial murderers, the youngest being Peter Woodcock, who was only 17 years old while he was active in the country. Legebokoff was condemned to life in prison without the possibility of release for 25 years in 2014. Cody Legebokoff was moved from British Columbia's maximum-security Kent Institution to Ontario's medium-security Warkworth Institution in 2019.

Cody Legebokoff was born in Fort St. James, British Columbia, on January 21, 1990. Both of his parents reared him. He has one or more brothers or sisters.

He finished 12 years of school and earned his high school diploma. He never had a wife. He didn't have any children. He has committed crimes before his crime spree.

Cody Legebokoff began his murdering rampage in 2009 (Age 18/19), and he was known to rape and murder his victims during his crimes as a serial killer. He resided with three close female friends in Prince George, where he was known to work as a serial murderer at the time of his murders.

He was arrested on November 28, 2010 (Age 20), convicted on September 11, 2014 (Age 24), and sentenced to life in prison without the possibility of release for 25 years in the Warkworth Institution in Ontario, Canada.

The Assaults

The last time anyone saw Jill Stuchenko alive was on October 9, 2009. While most Canadians were enjoying their Thanksgiving feasts, Jill was dying a terrible death. Four days later, her body was recovered in a gravel pit on the outskirts of Prince George.

Jill, a mother of six, works for an escort agency. She had visited an addiction treatment clinic only a few days before her death. An acquaintance testified that she was desperate to quit crack but kept relapsing every time she tried. Additional witnesses testified that Legebokoff purchased, sold, and smoked crack himself.

Jill died as a result of severe blunt force injuries to the head. Bruises from similar strikes were seen on her forehead, arms, and knees as well. She had lost so much blood that the forensic team had difficulty obtaining a sample for examination.

The postmortem results, which included DNA analysis of samples obtained from under her fingernail and swabs from her vagina and anus, indicated that the offender was an unknown male. A DNA sample obtained from Cody Legebokoff following his capture in November 2010 matched the Stuchenko samples. DNA extracted from Legebokoff's bloodstained sofa matched DNA extracted from what remained of Stuchenko's blood.

The jury determined after reviewing the evidence that Legebokoff killed Jill in the basement of his apartment during the Thanksgiving weekend of 2009 when his housemates were gone for the holiday. Cody Legebokoff was just 19 years old at the time of the first murder.

Natasha Lynn Montgomery, 23, vanished between August 30 and September 1, 2010. She left behind a son and a daughter. She and her long-term lover Godwin, their father, had broken up owing to her drug addiction. Despite this, they stayed in touch, and the kids phoned him every other day.

Although Natasha's corpse was never recovered, several things found in Legebokoff's apartment proved positive for her DNA, including clothing, an ax, a blanket, and bed linens. The jury determined after reviewing the evidence that Natasha Lynn Montgomery was brutally murdered at Legebokoff's apartment. They also determined that the ax was used, maybe in conjunction with other weapons, to either murder her or dispose of her corpse.

Cynthia Mass was discovered dead by two police officers patrolling L.C. Gunn Park on October 9, 2010. Her pants had been rolled all the way down to her knees, and her body had been dragged up to the tree line. She had received blunt force injuries as well as puncture lesions to her chest. She also sustained multiple broken ribs and fractures in her neck, cheekbone, right wrist, wrists, and two fingers. Dr.

Symes, the medical examiner, also observed five dull imprints on the left and top of her head.

A woman's black sweater was discovered behind the driver's seat of Legebokoff's truck during the inquiry. It, like a white sock recovered in the vehicle, had DNA from both Legebokoff and Cynthia. Following searches of Legebokoff's flat, a pair of black shoes and a pickaxe were discovered, both of which tested positive for Cynthia's and Legebokoff's DNA. After reviewing the evidence, the jury determined that Legebokoff killed Cynthia with the pickaxe.

Loren Leslie, born on January 5, 1995, developed into a visually handicapped 15-year-old who died late in the evening on November 27, 2010.

Cameron Hill, a conservation officer, discovered her corpse about midnight the same night, concealed in dense bushes by the side of an old logging road off Highway 27 near Fort St. James. Her jeans were rolled down to her ankles, and her body was arranged in a manner eerily identical to Cynthia's, which had been discovered some six weeks previously.

Unlike the other three incidents, the Leslie inquiry began immediately. Police had considerably more specific evidence regarding the events leading up to Loren's murder, and they had already identified Legebokoff as a major suspect.

Loren died due to a combination of blood loss from two knife wounds in her neck and brain damage from a series of massive strikes to the head that caused significant blunt force trauma. Cody Legebokoff's shirt, shorts, and shoes were stained with her blood and DNA.

There was also a lot of additional evidence in this case. Loren and Legebokoff's connection was revealed through a series of email and text messages that began on November 1, 2010. Loren's phone was discovered in the pocket of Legebokoff's shorts, along with a Leatherman multi-tool smeared with her blood. A bloodied pipe wrench that tested positive for Loren's DNA was discovered on the floor of Legebokoff's truck, along with her wallet, I.D., and bag.

Using one glance at this huge pile of incriminating evidence, the jurors determined that Loren Leslie was killed with the pipe wrench and the Leatherman tool.

The Trial

Amy Voell, Legebokoff's former girlfriend, testified that she slept overnight at his 1400-block Liard Drive residence three to four times a week. She remembered seeing a bloody handprint on a wall near the front entrance, as well as crimson stains on the living room drapes and a carpet at the end of the corridor. There was also blood on the couch, but Amy didn't make it a point to mention it.

When she inquired about the sanguinary stains, Legebokoff informed her that his own blood caused them. He'd made a shambles of himself while high, and he'd suffered a nosebleed, which explained the blood on the curtain.

Amy informed authorities that they had both worked that day, but Legebokoff's shift had ended before hers. Amy got off and drove to Legebokoff's place, where they rested and watched TV. She departed about 6:30 p.m.

because Legebokoff was really tired, and it was the last time she saw him.

On August 26 and 27, 2014, Legebokoff testified before the jury, informing them of the presence of three people he named as X, Y, and Z, who he said had played a significant role in the killings of Jill Stuchenko, Cynthia Maas, and Natasha Montgomery. (It would have been too ridiculous to attempt to put Loren Leslie's murder on them as well, so he didn't.) During his evidence, Legebokoff stated unequivocally that he would not be providing the entire truth since he would not tell the court who X, Y, and Z were.

According to Legebokoff, he met drug supplier X regularly from the end of August until October 10, 2009, a period of around six weeks. X had become acquainted with Legebokoff and trusted him enough to bring his victims to his home for execution. X mistook Legebokoff for a participant in the assassinations. While Legebokoff claimed that he had not done so, he had been a reasonably gracious host. He not only allowed the killings to take place in his home, but he also supplied the equipment. On the other hand, Cynthia had been murdered not by X at Legebokoff's apartment but by Y in L.C. Gunn Park—with the pickaxe given by Legebokoff.

The main difficulty with Legebokoff's account was that there was no independent proof that X, Y, and Z existed. The heinous three appeared to have swept through the crime scenes without leaving a trace of DNA evidence—neither on clothing, murder weapons, or the two bodies discovered. The jury found that Legebokoff made up these nameless and faceless persons out of thin air.

Furthermore, Legebokoff said that X, Y, and Z were responsible for one of the killings. This appeared especially strange given that they had all allegedly been present for all of the killings. However, a thorough analysis of Legebokoff's evidence revealed that no more than one individual attacked any of the victims at any time. Legebokoff, for example, said that he and Y merely sat around while X assaulted the victims and struggled with Natasha for almost five minutes.

Finally, on September 16, 2014, Cody Legebokoff was sentenced to life in prison without the possibility of release for 25 years.

Leopold Dion

On that lovely spring day in April 1963, Leopold Dion was already a convicted sex offender when he advanced to murder. He had, in fact, recently been freed from prison for raping a young schoolteacher. Other crimes, such as 21 rapes and horrific gang rape of a young lady (committed with his brother), had gone unnoticed by authorities. That person had likewise been stabbed and left for dead on the railroad lines outside the Quebec town of Pont-Rouge. She survived but was traumatized and unable to identify her assailants, allowing Dion to go on a murdering rampage.

Guy Luckenuck, a 12-year-old musical protégée, was Dion's first victim. Guy left his house early on April 20, 1963, to attend a piano lesson at the Quebec City Conservatory. He was finished by two o'clock that afternoon and, with time on his hands, decided to visit the Plains of Abraham, a memorial place inside

Battlefields Park. It was there when he ran into a beaming Leopold Dion.

Dion was wearing a camera around his neck and pretended to be a photojournalist for an American magazine. He asked Guy whether he'd mind posing for some photos, and the child consented. However, after taking a few photos, Dion announced that the location would not be enough. He then asked Guy if he wanted to go into the country with him to capture some more photographs. Again, the youngster had no protest, and they were driving away in Dion's automobile seconds later.

Dion stopped the car to the side of the road between the villages of St. Augustine and St. Catherine and instructed Guy to get out. There were some low dunes nearby, so he took a couple of photos with them as a backdrop. Then, all of a sudden, his mood shifted, and he motioned Guy to remove his clothing.

When Dion grew forceful, the youngster first refused, then began to weep. He eventually attempted to flee, but Dion was faster and stronger. He pushed Guy to the ground and began strangling him, applying pressure on his throat until the boy's breathing ceased. Dion then casually strolled back to his car to fetch a spade, which he used to bury Guy in a small hole in the dunes.

Guy Luckenuck's disappearance made quite a stir in Quebec City. However, the authorities had only just begun to investigate the case when two more youngsters went missing. On May 5, 1963, Alain Carrier, eight, and Michel Morel, 10, were walking near Quebec's famed Chateau Frontenac when they were approached by a man who offered them money to pose for photographs. The guys agreed and traveled to Saint-Raymond-de-Portneuf with the pleasant photographer to a run-down cottage. Dion informed them that he wanted one of the lads to pose as a prisoner for the picture session. Dion then tied Alain up inside the cottage before escorting Michel outdoors. Dion insisted that Michel remove his clothing as he had done with Guy Luckenuck. When the boy shook, he wrapped a nail-studded garrote around his neck and tightened it around him, keeping pressure on him until Michel collapsed on the floor. Dion then took up a rock and began beating Michel's head until all that remained was a jumble of shattered bone and bleeding brain tissue.

Dion strolled back to his car and returned with a burlap sack, now that the elder boy was out of the way. Ignoring Alain's frantic pleas, the callous killer pulled the sack over the kid's head and kept it there until the youngster suffocated. Alain and Michel were laid to rest in a small cemetery.

Dion waited just three weeks before performing his next heinous act. The 26th of May was another beautiful day in Quebec. Pierre Marquis, thirteen, had gone to Anse-au-Foulon beach with friends and started a discussion with Dion at some time during the morning. Dion used his now-familiar ploy to offer the youngster money in exchange for posing for pictures. Pierre nodded and followed him towards the dunes. When Dion requested him to pose naked, he consented but resisted and pushed back when Dion began caressing him. The tiny adolescent, though, was no match for the huge 250-pound Dion. He was quickly defeated and strangled to death, his body being buried in the dunes.

By this point, the Quebec police were concerned that they could be dealing with a serial murderer who preyed on young boys. And, with no proof, they readied themselves for another child murder in the following weeks. Given the killer's extraordinary rate of murdering his young victims, this appeared virtually unavoidable.

But then the cops got a fortunate break. A woman took her kid into a Quebec police station the day after the Marquis murder to describe a terrible experience. A guy approached the child when he was playing alone and offered him money to pose for pictures. They had gone to an isolated location when the guy became violent and demanded that the youngster remove his clothing. Fortunately, the quick-footed lad was able to outrun his adversary and make a break for it. When shown a photo array, the youngster correctly identified Leopold Dion as the photographer. Dion was arrested the next day.

Dion was now being held on an attempted kidnapping accusation by the police. But if they believed he was going to confess to murder, they were dead wrong. He resisted all his interrogators could throw at him for a whole month and maintained his innocence unwaveringly. He eventually broke down and confessed to murdering the four youngsters. He later took detectives to the locations where the children's remains were buried.

Prosecutors ultimately chose to charge Dion with only one murder, that of Pierre Marquis, since they felt it would be the simplest to establish. As it turned out, one murder was more than enough for their goals. Dion was found guilty on April 10, 1964, and sentenced to death by hanging. The Governor-General of Canada, Georges Vanier, eventually reduced that sentence to life imprisonment. Fate, on the other hand, had different ideas for Leopold Dion.

On November 17, 1972, Dion was assaulted by fellow convict Norman Champagne, a person with schizophrenia who believed he was acting on orders from Lawrence of Arabia. Dion was stabbed to death and disfigured terribly. He seemed to have maintained his appointment with the executioner after all.

Gilbert Paul Jordan

We've all heard about serial murderers, and many of us are familiar with their most prevalent murder techniques. Some strangle their victims, while others stab them or beat them with blunt items. Gilbert Paul Jordan, AKA the Boozing Barber, deserves credit for one of the most inventive and least suspect tactics. Jordan drank his victims until they were nearly unconscious, then murdered them by pushing them to drink still more.

Jordan was linked to the murders of eight to ten women in Vancouver, British Columbia, between 1965 and 1988, and he may have been involved in dozens of more fatalities that were not directly related to him. He was the first known Canadian to utilize booze as a murder weapon. He was also a heavy drinker who regularly hired Native prostitutes on Vancouver's Downtown Eastside to join him for a few—well, many—drinks. Jordan would continue to pour vodka or other alcoholic beverages down their throats until they died.

His lengthy criminal record included rape, indecent assault, drunk driving, hit-and-run, and car theft. These occurred prior to his arrest for the "alcohol killings," He was sentenced to six years in prison for manslaughter.

Dr. Tibor Bezeredi diagnosed Jordan with an antisocial personality disorder after a court-ordered psychiatric assessment in 1976. According to Dr. Bezeredi, Jordan is "a person whose behavior is maladjusted in terms of social behavior; disdain for the rights of others, which frequently ends in criminal acts."

Jordan passed away in 2006.

Childhood

Jordan was born on December 12, 1931, in Vancouver. Gilbert Paul Elsie was his birth name. By the age of 16, he had become an alcoholic and had dropped out of high school. By 21, he had accumulated a lengthy criminal record that included rape, violence, theft, and heroin possession.

Jordan had an insatiable desire for booze and drunk sex. He was an uncontrollable drinker who frequently drank more than three pints of vodka each day. As a matter of necessity, he sought out the companionship of other alcoholics. "I didn't want to drink in my room all by myself," he stated during his trial, and sober individuals wouldn't have anything to do with him, so he had no alternative but to hang out with other alcoholics.

He also claimed to have sex with over 200 women every year. He looked for prostitutes in Vancouver's slums, low-rent pubs, and seedy dives.

Jordan was frequently found to be on the wrong side of the law. In 1961, he was arrested in his automobile with a five-year-old Aboriginal child and accused of abduction. However, the case was halted by a stay of proceedings in May 1961, and he was never convicted.

Jordan threatened to leap over the Lions Gate Bridge in a drunken state just after Christmas that year. Traffic came to a stop until he was persuaded to back up. He was punished for contempt of court not long after when he made a Nazi salute in a North Vancouver courtroom.

Jordan invited two women to drink with him in his vehicle in 1963. He raped them and took their stuff when they were intoxicated. He was accused of rape and theft, but although being convicted of stealing, he was acquitted of rape owing to a lack of evidence.

Jordan proceeded to sexually abuse defenseless women regularly, which resulted in his spending time in and out of jail. He trained to be a barber during one of his numerous jail sentences, and when he was released, he opened the Slocan Barber Shop on Kingsway Avenue on Vancouver's filthy Downtown Eastside. He also inherited some money, which he put into the stock market.

Soon after, the Boozing Barber added murder to his lengthy list of transgressions. His investments had yielded a profit. He could afford a decent attorney.

Killings

Jordan's first victim was English-born, but his subsequent victims were all Native women from the notorious Downtown Eastside. His tactic was to pursue Native American prostitutes at dingy bars. He'd give the women money in exchange for sex and company and take them to his run-down barbershop or a cheap hotel room. He'd urge them to drink with him and give them extra money if they could drink straight booze. When they passed out, he'd pour more vodka down their throats and rape them as they died.

Jordan, a strong drinker, fit in well with the locals in the pubs he visited. He came across like a milquetoast compared to the burnt-out addicts and prostitutes crowding about him, with a bald head, thick black-rimmed glasses, and a short and stocky body. Nobody would ever think of him as threatening; thus, it was very easy for him to entice ladies who appeared to be "on their last legs." These ladies, like him, were drinkers who did not hang out with the drug scene. They liked free drinks and quickly agreed to Jordan's proposals.

Jordan was equally as haphazard in his choice of mates. During a deposition, he claimed, "I didn't care who I was with." I mean, whether it's at this bar, across the street, or elsewhere, we're all going to die sooner or later."

Despite his lowlife ways, Jordan had acquired a sizable inheritance and made prudent investments, the profits from which enabled him to employ the best lawyers.

Despite his multiple offenses, he was not designated a Dangerous Offender for many years. But everything changed when the rapes and attacks escalated into killings.

One night in 1965, Ivy Rose (Doreen) Oswald, a switchboard operator, joined Jordan on one of his drinking sprees. The next day, her nude body was discovered in a Vancouver hotel room. Her blood alcohol concentration was revealed to be 0.51.

In most countries, the legal driving limit is 0.08, while mortality from alcohol poisoning generally occurs at a level of about 0.4. A dozen drinks would result in a blood alcohol level of about 0.3, at which time the drinker would most likely pass out. To die from alcohol poisoning, the drinker would have to consume a massive amount of alcohol in a short period.

Nonetheless, Doreen's death was ruled an accident, and the matter was closed. Her assassin confessed to the crime 22 years later.

Charges and Convictions Subsequently.

Gilbert Paul Elsie applied to alter his surname to Jordan soon after his first murder. The request was approved.

Jordan proceeded to rack up charges and convictions under his new identity, several for drunk driving. He was even prosecuted twice in one day in 1969. Among the other criminal charges filed during this period were:

- Engaging in an obscene act in a public location (1971, Vancouver)
- Incestuous exposure (1973, Mackenzie)
- Incestuous assault (1974, Prince George)

He was convicted of the 1974 crime and sentenced to nearly two years in prison. The Crown was working hard by this point to have Jordan labeled a Dangerous

Offender, but his lawyers were able to get the motion refused.

He returned to his old ways as soon as he was released from prison in 1975. He abducted and raped a mentally disabled lady from a mental facility the same year, feeling no shame or remorse. If the court wanted proof that Jordan was a dangerous sex offender, here was it. Even if he hadn't committed any other crimes, this alone should have been enough to put him in and toss away the key.

This heinous conduct landed him in jail on many charges, including kidnapping and sexual intercourse with a vulnerable victim. However, the court did not consider his past offenses and treated him more leniently than he deserved. He received just a 26-month sentence for this heinous act, which had devastating consequences when he was released and embarked on a murdering spree that took the lives of numerous more women.

Three women died at Slocan Barber Shop on Kingsway Avenue between July 1982 and June 1985. Jordan reported each of these incidents after speaking with his lawyer, but he was not investigated. The coroner in each case reported that the lady died of alcohol poisoning, and because they were all known drinkers, they were all at great danger of the same destiny. Add to it the fact that all three were prostitutes, and it's easy to see why the cops were so unconcerned about their deaths.

Jordan was also linked to the murders of three Aboriginal women who were discovered dead in separate motel rooms. Jordan had been with six different ladies at the time of their deaths:

- On November 30, 1980, Mary Johnson at the Aylmer Hotel with a Blood Alcohol Level of 0.34.
- On September 11, 1981, Barbara Paul at the Glenaird Hotel with a Blood Alcohol Level of 0.41

- On July 30, 1982, Mary Johns at Slocan Barbershop with a Blood Alcohol Level of 0.76

- On December 15, 1984, Patricia Thomas at Slocan Barbershop with a Blood Alcohol Level of 0.51.

Allan Legere

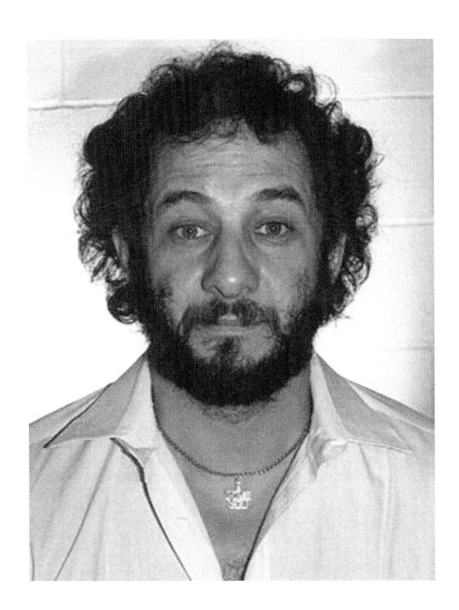

Allan Legere was born in Chatham Falls, New Brunswick, on February 13, 1948. At the time of his birth, his mother Louise already had three children, all of whom were fathered by a violent drinker called Vincent Legere, who had long ago abandoned the family. On the other hand, Allan's father was Lionel Comeau, a ne'er-do-well who had an affair with Louise.

The Legere family lived on the outskirts of destitution, which was aggravated when Lionel Comeau abandoned Louise, leaving her to raise four children on her own. More tragedy came in 1956 when Allan's older brother Freddy was killed in a vehicle accident. Allan was nine years old at the time. Louise would continuously tell him from then on that she wished he had died instead of Freddy.

One can only imagine how such news must have affected a nine-year-old. In Allan's case, despite his evident brilliance, it caused him to become exceedingly reclusive and do poorly in school. It also pushed him to his first instances of anti-social conduct.

When Legere was 16, he began entering residences, sometimes burglarizing them and occasionally fondling sleeping female inhabitants. Between 1964 and 1966, he was arrested twice and spent 18 months in jail. Then, in 1969, he appeared to settle down after marrying a nurse and fathering two children with her. For a while, Legere and his small family relocated to North Bay, Ontario, but by 1972, they were back in Miramichi, where he found employment in a sawmill. After being caught for possessing stolen items and sentenced to five months in jail, he was fired from his work. His wife grabbed the children and fled to Ottawa shortly after he finished that tenure.

Legere was questioned in 1974 about the horrific death of Chatham Head resident Beatrice Mary Redmond. Mrs. Redmond was on her way home from church when she was assaulted and stabbed more than 80 times. Legere was considered a strong suspect, but no concrete evidence was found against him, and he was never prosecuted. Perhaps that close encounter terrified him since Legere managed to keep off the radar of law enforcement for the following decade. All of that changed in 1986.

On Saturday, June 21, 1986, Legere and two teenage accomplices broke into the house of 66-year-old John Glendenning and his wife Mary, startling the elderly couple sitting in front of the television. Mr. Glendenning was bludgeoned with a rock by one of the invaders, who then dragged his wife into the kitchen, where she was tied to a chair and severely abused. One of the males began fondling her after ripping her clothes and panties. Meanwhile, the others began assaulting her husband and demanding the safe combination. Mary assured the assailants she would unlock the safe to protect John from further harm. She was brought upstairs, but she hadn't even started spinning the knobs when she was knocked out by two strikes to the back of the head.

Mary Glendenning awoke in the toilet bowl with her head in it. Every part of her body appeared to be screaming in pain, yet she managed to drag herself to the telephone in the bedroom and dial 911. Within minutes, an ambulance and a Royal Canadian Mounted Police unit arrived on the scene. Mrs. Glendenning had been battered so brutally that one of her lungs had collapsed at Chatham's Hotel Dieu Hospital. She had been raped with a blunt instrument as well. But, at the very least, she was alive. John, her spouse, was not so fortunate. He'd been strangled and battered to death.

An arrest was made quickly. Allan Legere, 38, Scott Curtis, 20, and Todd Matchett, 18, were detained three days after the incident. Curtis and Matchett immediately admitted their guilt, describing Legere as the ringleader.

Allan Legere was convicted guilty of second-degree murder on January 8, 1987. He was condemned to life in jail with no chance of release for the next 18 years. He had no intention of finishing the statement.

Legere had been with the company for just over two years when he decided to leave. He was transferred from the Atlantic Institute Prison in Renous, New Brunswick, to Dumont Hospital in Moncton on Wednesday, May 3, 1989, to treat a chronic ear infection. He requested to use the restroom while in the hospital and was granted permission to do so. In handcuffs and leg shackles, Legere entered the restroom. He emerged moments later, the shackles released, and ran past his astonished guards. A frenzied pursuit occurred through the hospital and out into the parking lot, where Legere approached and kidnapped a female driver's vehicle. The woman was eventually freed unhurt. Legere, on the other hand, was long gone.

A massive manhunt was started, but the police were no closer to apprehending the fugitive after a month of hunting. They believed he'd departed the province, if not the nation. They were mistaken.

On the morning of May 29, 1989, a Chatham homeowner observed smoke billowing from her next-door neighbor's window. She quickly dialed 911, and the fire department arrived to smash down the rear door and enter the house. They discovered Nina Flam, terribly burnt but still alive, at the bottom of the stairs. She was airlifted to a hospital in Fredericton while firemen were forced to flee the property due to the blazing blaze within. When the flames were finally put out, they discovered another body, this one charred practically to ash. Nina's sister-in-law, Annie Flam, was 75 years old. Annie was a well-known local character, and her grocery shop had been a fixture in the community for almost 50 years.

When Nina Flam was well enough to talk with police, she informed them what had transpired. A masked guy had broken into the house in the middle of the night, raped both elderly ladies, and then beaten them to death.

Another older adult was attacked on Saturday night, September 30, this time in nearby Newcastle. Morrissey Doran, 70, was shot in the back of the head with a shotgun but survived. A day later, 75-year-old Sonny Russell confronted a guy with a shotgun who was attempting to break into his home. Despite his old years, Russell was able to beat the guy off, prompting him to escape. By the time the police arrived, there had been reports of another attempted break-in at Billy Matchett's house. Mr. Matchett was the father of Todd, one of Legere's Glendenning murder conspirators. This gave the police information on the individual they were looking for. They were now confident that Allan Legere was responsible for the wave of attacks.

Meanwhile, the press picked up on the tale and splashed headlines about the "Monster of the Miramichi." Despite the mayor's calls for calm, the little village went into a frenzy, with gun purchases skyrocketing.

A volunteer firefighter observed smoke coming from a two-story residence in Newcastle, New Brunswick, on Saturday, October 14, 1989. He quickly alerted his colleagues, who raced into the home in search of survivors. Donna Daughney, 41, was discovered on the bed in an upper bedroom. Linda, 45, was lying near her on the floor. Neither of the women was breathing. An autopsy eventually revealed that they'd both been brutally battered, with Donna dying to her wounds and Linda surviving only to die of smoke inhalation. They'd both been raped.

The RCMP presence in the region was increased in the weeks after the Daughney double killing. Meanwhile, journalists from all across the country were flocking to the quiet town, like sharks to a sinking ship. Allan Legere gave them something to write about on November 16.

Worshippers came to the Church of the Blessed Virgin in Chatham Head at approximately 7 p.m. on that day for the 7 p.m. service. They were taken aback to see the church deserted and dark. When no response was received from the elderly padre, Father James Smith, one of the parishioners, decided to enter the rectory to investigate. He was taken aback and reeled back. The interior of the house was in chaos, with smashed furniture and shattered glass. And there was blood all over the place, covering the walls and the floor.

The cops arrived quickly and saw the 69-year-old clergyman lying on the ground. He'd been beaten mercilessly, and it was clear that he'd been tortured before dying. His face had deep cuts slashed into it, and his ribs had caved in. An autopsy would reveal that he died as a result of choking on his own vomit.

Following the murder of Father Smith, the police increased their search for Legere. He had escaped to Montreal, where he had remained until Thursday, November 23. On that frigid evening in Saint John, New Brunswick, he waved down Ron Gomke, a 21-year-old cab driver. Legere pulled out a pistol and told Gomke to drive to Chatham. He then informed the surprised cabbie who he was and that he intended to hijack a plane and go to Iran.

Unfortunately for Legere, his escape plot went bad nearly right away. Gomke lost control of the cab and skidded into a ditch just outside of Moncton. Legere was rescued from the stranded car by a female driver who happened to be an off-duty RCMP officer. When he took out a gun and told her she had to go to Chatham, she stated she needed to stop at a gas station first. She was able to give him the slip and drive away, leaving him stranded. The officer called for backup, but as a swarm of cops arrived, Legere made one last desperate effort for freedom, forcing trucker Brian Golding into his car and ordering him to drive.

Golding did what he was ordered, but only a few miles later, he slammed on the brakes, hurling Legere forward. He then leaped out of the car and fled. Legere was apprehended shortly afterward.

Allan Legere went on trial at the Fredericton courthouse on August 26, 1991, charged with four counts of murder. Two days later, the jury returned a unanimous guilty verdict, and the judge handed down a sentence of life in prison. Legere is currently incarcerated at the Special Handling Unit of the Sainte-Anne-des-Plaines Prison in Montreal. It is highly unlikely that he will ever be released.

Melissa Ann Friedrich

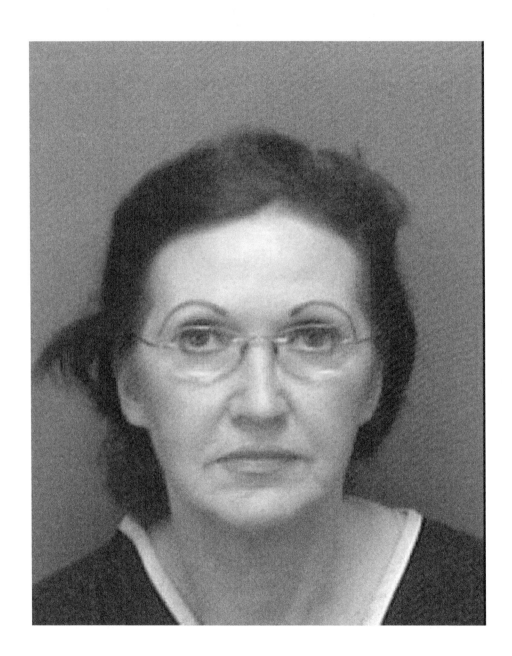

Black widows and Bluebeards are widely regarded as financially motivated assassins. Their standard operating procedure is to trick unsuspecting victims into marrying them (often in secret) and then handing away all they own. After that, the victim is quickly killed before the murderer moves on to their next "project." However, the majority of these assassins had another purpose. They revel in the excitement of the chase, entangling the victim in a web of falsehoods and watching as they hurtle unknowingly into their demise. It's comparable to pretending to be God.

Melissa Ann Stewart was born on May 16, 1938, in Burnt Church, New Brunswick. She went to Ontario with her family as a youngster, where she met and married manufacturing worker Russell Sheppard in 1955. Melissa was just 17 at the time, yet she left her family behind to relocate to Montague, Prince Edward Island, with her new husband. She had two children, a boy and a daughter, by the age of 20. She had also broken the law for the first time, receiving an 11-month prison sentence for forgery. She would be imprisoned for one-third of the following 15 years on different fraud and forgery offenses.

Predictably, Melissa's proclivity for small criminality put a strain on her marriage, and the pair divorced. She moved in with widower Gordon Stewart in 1988 and subsequently married him in twin ceremonies in Las Vegas and Vancouver. Stewart had no idea the marriage was null and void. His bride was still wedded to her previous husband and would not divorce him until May 1991.

That wasn't the only thing Gordon Stewart didn't know about his new bride. When money began to disappear from Gordon's bank accounts, the couple had just moved into their new home in Vancouver, British Columbia. Melissa began accusing her husband of sexual and physical abuse around the same time.

Gordon Stewart was hospitalized to a Vancouver hospital just before Christmas 1990. He was confused and frothing at the lips. Doctors quickly found why. He'd taken a lot of benzodiazepine, a psychotropic medication that's generally recommended for sleeplessness or anxiety. Stewart maintained he wasn't using the drug, but he ultimately recovered and the issue was dropped. A few months later, police were summoned to the Stewart residence for a domestic dispute. Gordon was arrested for assault after a brief inquiry. He was sentenced to three weeks in prison after pleading guilty to the crime.

When Gordon was freed in March 1991, he discovered that Melissa had gotten a restraining order against him. He defied the rule and hunted down Melissa, pleading with her to take him back. She eventually consented, and the pair relocated to Dartmouth, Nova Scotia, in April. Their reconciliation would be short-lived.

Melissa Stewart loaded her husband with wine and benzodiazepine on April 27, 1991, one year after their wedding, drove him out to a lonely stretch of road near Halifax Airport, pushed him out of the vehicle, and ran him over. She then backed up and reversed over him, according to two eyewitnesses, as he lay on the blacktop.

Melissa drove home and changed her clothing after leaving Gordon's corpse where it had fallen, before phoning the police three hours later. She claimed that Gordon had abused and raped her throughout their marriage during her trial, citing "battered wife syndrome." This seems to be taken into account by the jury. They convicted Melissa of manslaughter despite proof of a fatal amount of benzodiazepine detected in Gordon's system. She received a six-year jail term. She only serviced two people.

Melissa Stewart discovered a new technique to search for unfortunate victims as the new century started -

the Internet. She began investigating dating sites, particularly Christian dating websites geared toward seniors. In April 2000, she met retired engineer Robert Friedrich through this means. Friedrich offered her to visit him at his house in Florida a month after they began emailing. During their first meeting, she said unequivocally that she thought God wanted them to be together. Within three days, they were planning their wedding. They married a month later in Dartmouth, Nova Scotia. Melissa then moved to Bradenton, Florida, to live with her new spouse.

It wasn't long after the wedding that Robert Friedrich's family noticed a shift in his demeanor. His health deteriorated, and he began to slur his speech. The family suspected Melissa, and one of Friedrich's sons even filed a complaint with the Elder Abuse Line in July 2002. Friedrich died six months later after an alleged heart attack. During his two-year marriage to

Melissa, he designated her as the only beneficiary of his $100,000 fortune.

Unsurprisingly, Robert Friedrich's family was skeptical of the circumstances surrounding his death. They filed a complaint with the county sheriff, saying that Melissa poisoned him. Unfortunately, there was no way to prove this because the corpse had been cremated. Melissa lived in Florida for the following two years, cashing her husband's social security payments. In the meantime, a legal suit had robbed her of everything but $15,000 from Robert Friedrich's inheritance.

Melissa returned to Canada in 2004, but before the end of the year, she was back in Florida, pursuing Alex Strategos, a 73-year-old man she met online. She followed him back to his Pinellas Park apartment on the night of their first date and declared that she was moving in. Soon after, a familiar pattern emerged. Strategos began to have dizzy episodes, slurred speech, and little mishaps. Over the following three months, he was brought to the emergency room eight times. Melissa convinced him to grant her power of attorney over his financial affairs during one of those trips. She then began withdrawing funds from his accounts.

Fortunately, Alex Strategos' son was not duped by Melissa's smooth words. Dean Strategos went to the police after discovering that benzodiazepine had been detected in his father's blood tests and that there had been many big withdrawals from his father's bank account. Melissa Friedrich was arrested and charged with grand theft, fraud, and forgery on January 6, 2005. She accepted a plea deal and received a five-year jail term.

Melissa was freed from a Florida jail and deported to Canada in 2009. In Nova Scotia, she moved into a senior complex. Even at the age of 74, she wasn't finished. She was soon scouring dating websites for another dinner ticket. Fred Weeks, 75, was the one she discovered.

Weeks married Melissa on September 25, 2012, but he barely survived the honeymoon period. On September 28, the couple arrived at a guesthouse in North Sydney, Nova Scotia, and retreated to their room. Melissa informed the staff the next morning that her husband was unwell and needed an ambulance. She, on the other hand, insisted on completing her meal before the paramedics arrived. Fred Weeks, who was weak and disoriented, was discovered on the floor of the couple's room by paramedics. He was transported to the hospital, where testing revealed that he had a significant amount of benzodiazepine in his system. He later recovered completely.

Melissa's cache, which included 144 Lorazepam tablets and numerous other medications prescribed by five different doctors, was discovered during a search of the Weeks home.

Melissa consented to a three-year jail sentence after being charged with the attempted murder of her fourth husband. Meanwhile, American and Canadian officials look into her for tens of thousands of dollars in social security fraud.

Conclusion

Canada has long been a nation of contrasts, with bustling hubs of modern industry juxtaposed against huge expanses of desolate waste in the far north. It's no accident that most of the country's metropolitan population centers are located around its southern border: despite Canada's vast territory, over 90 percent of it is barren tundra.

Only the bravest of hearts live in the extreme north, and for the vast majority of Canadians, their country runs in a small livable zone stretching from Vancouver in the west to Montreal in the east. This belt is densely populated, yet a few miles north can lead you to a nearly deserted wilderness. Perhaps it is Canada's vast, frigid north that permits so many murderers to thrive. Many of them, like Robert Pickton, have hunted their prey in cities before retreating to secluded lairs in the cold wastelands.

McArthur, too, is accused of picking up his victims in the urban jungle of Toronto's Gay Village before burying their mutilated bodies beyond the wide Canadian frontier. Then there's Russell Williams, a Colonel in the Canadian Forces who teaches cadets how to save lives by day while working hard to murder them by night. The most infamous serial murderers in Canada come in various forms and sizes.

Printed in Great Britain
by Amazon

76914734R00081